TOP 10 BOND MARKET WORRIES

By Marilyn Cohen and Chris Malburg

Also by Marilyn Cohen and Chris Malburg

The Great Unravel
The Little Bond eBook
Surviving the Bond Bear Market: Bondland's Nuclear Winter
Bonds Now!
The Bond Bible

* * *

Top 10 Bond Market Worries

By Marilyn Cohen and **Chris** Malburg

Published by Marilyn Cohen and Chris Malburg at Amazon
All rights reserved
Copyright 2018 by Marilyn Cohen and Chris Malburg
Amazon Edition

This eBook is licensed for your personal enjoyment only. This eBook may not be re-sold or given away to others. If you would like to share this book, please purchase an additional copy for each recipient. If you are reading this book and did not purchase it, or it was not purchased for your use only, then please return to Amazon.com and purchase your own copy. Thank you for respecting the hard work of this author.

Library of Congress Cataloging-in-Publication Data
Cohen, Marilyn and Malburg, Chris
The Great Unravel/ Marilyn Cohen Chris Malburg
ISBN-13: 978-1727349795
ISBN-10: 1727349792
1. Bonds. 2. Interest rates. 3. Yield 4. Marilyn Cohen 5. Chris Malburg. 6. Municipal bonds 7. Corporate bonds 8. Bond yield

* * * *

Table of Content

Welcome to *Top 10 Bond Market Worries* 1

Chapter 1: Death Star Amazon 2
   Amazon's fulfillment centers 2
   Expanding Amazon's reach with Whole Foods 2
   Amazon's impact on municipalities 2
   Defending against the Amazon Death Star 3

Chapter 2: Unfunded Pensions 5
   What's the danger to bonds? 5
   No safe haven 5
   When the unthinkable happens 6
   Beware Pension Obligation Bonds 7

Chapter 3: Confiscatory Taxation of Americans 8
   State and local government's nasty habit 8
   California's communications tax 8
   How you pay your estimated tax matters 8
   What SALT did 9
   Taxing devices 10
      Millionaire's tax 10
      Head tax 10
      Parcel tax 11
      Indirect taxes 11
   Wealth is portable 12

Chapter 4: Concentration Comes in Many Forms 13
   Airport revenue bonds 13
   Over reliance on one company or industry 13
   Exit King James 14
   One huge cost 15
   Overcoming over concentration 15

Chapter 5: Shots Fired in Treasury Market 17
   What about a possible credit crisis? 17
   What's the right allocation? 18
   The Fed is reducing its balance sheet 18
   Keeping our Asian creditors happy 19
      Consequences of China reducing its US Treasury purchases 19

Chapter 6: The negatives of corporate-issued debt 21
- Reading the fine print 22
- The fallacy of add-backs 22
- How to buy corporate bonds 23

Chapter 7: Everybody into the Bond Indexing Pool 24
- The indexing tsunami 24
- Undue concentration 24
- Indexing defenses 25

Chapter 8: Technological Disruptors 27
- Artificial intelligence as a disruptor 27
- Augmented reality as a disruptor 28
- New sales channels 28
- The Internet of things 29
- Embrace AI technology or die 29
- The opportunity of 5G 30

Chapter 9: The bond binge is over—now what? 32
- Corporate bond risk 33
- Deteriorating credit quality 33

Chapter 10: Actionable Intel 35
- Known knowns 35
- Known unknowns 36
- Unknown unknowns 37
- Specific actions for investors 38

About the authors 40
- Marilyn Cohen 40
- Chris Malburg 40

Connect with us online 41
A final word from the authors 41
Other books by Marilyn Cohen and Chris Malburg 41
About Envision Capital 41

Welcome to *Top 10 Bond Market Worries*

We bond managers are wired differently than equity managers. We are the financial markets' worrywarts. What do we worry about? Everything. What will drive a particular credit—corporate or municipal—off the rails? We study catalysts for downgrades, management *faux pas*, balance sheets, and coverage ratios. You name it and it's on our worry list.

This little booklet will increase your awareness of our Top 10 Bond Market Worries and will save you from getting trapped in unsafe bond positions.

While low interest rates put stocks, bonds, and real estate on an upward trajectory, little money actually seeped into the real economy. Throughout the Obama Administration, two percent and below GDP growth was the stubborn norm.

During the previous Administration, many of us wondered when the financial party would begin. What event would start the profits rolling? President Trump's policies could be the positive sea change bond investors have been looking for. This is not the only politically slanted note you will find in this pamphlet. We do not apologize for our bias. We believe in this Administration's strategy and tactics as related to the growing US economy.

Best wishes for profitable investing,

Marilyn Cohen & Chris Malburg

* * *

Chapter 1: Death Star Amazon

Why should a bond book spend time talking about just one company? And why single out Amazon as that target? Amazon provides the greatest value added for so much of everything it touches. This usually comes in the form of selection, price, quality, easy return policy, and unparalleled speed of delivery. Amazon's seismic moves shake the earth. The corporate as well as the municipal bond markets feel it.

Amazon's fulfillment centers

Amazon has fulfillment centers in 30 states. There is fierce competition among municipalities to attract Amazon fulfillment centers. The company buys up large parcels of land. They employ hundreds. These employees set up housekeeping, buy homes, and rent apartments. This creates sales tax revenue, property tax revenue, and adds to the purchase of durable goods. Their kids go to public schools. All of this is good for the municipal bond holders.

However, if the area is hugely dependent on just one employer—like Amazon—there's a risk. What happens if that benefactor decides to leave? Bonds dependent on these revenue streams could see prices tank and yields soar. In the worst case, the issuer may have no choice but to default, leaving investors holding the bag.

Expanding Amazon's reach with Whole Foods

Amazon has a deep and robust platform both in its online presence and with its 2017 acquisition of Whole Foods. It's not just for groceries. Amazon now can integrate other businesses into the same brick and mortar footprint—pharmacies is a good example with their PillPack acquisition.

Amazon's impact on municipalities

Amazon's ability to crush competitors not only impacts corporate bond investors, but it's relevant to municipal bond holders as well. Amazon has proven it can serve its customers faster, better, and cheaper than any competitor. Its presence can and does force the competition out of business.

In the pharmaceutical space the major competitors suffering at the hands of Amazon include Walgreens, CVS, and Rite Aid. For the grocery space, just pick your favorite market and see how Amazon will likely affect its longevity.

As Amazon discounts its products, competitors' profit margins shrink forcing them to shutter their doors. Of course the victims' corporate bond credit quality suffers. But it also has a domino effect on the municipality's revenue:

- People can't find work and leave the area
- Property tax revenue falls—municipal bonds are backed by property tax revenue
- The holders of the municipality's general obligation bonds will suffer as the shortfall taps into their reserves
- Student census at public schools drops, causing a shortfall in state reimbursement to the affected schools. Many of these school districts issued bonds
- Sales tax revenue falls—though some of it is recovered by Internet sales tax collections
- Employer payroll tax revenue falls
- Public employees will suffer as their wages, pension fund contributions, and health care benefits succumb to the fiscal pressure of too many needs chasing too few dollars

Any cash on hand these municipalities might have had dwindles away to cover fixed overhead and operating expenses that they cannot cut fast enough. The cost of borrowing soars from all these negatives. Soon the municipality is so deep in the hole it cannot dig its way out. Woe is to those investors who failed to see the impact Amazon has on their municipal bond portfolio.

Defending against the Amazon Death Star

All is not lost for corporate and municipal bond investors. There is a way to minimize the risk this company presents to your portfolio. First, let's identify how Amazon crushes its competitors.

Amazon integrates its various businesses both horizontally and vertically. Horizontally, Amazon has the potential to take over an entire industry—such as pharmaceutical distribution.

Vertically, Amazon may choose to enter a business such as blue jean manufacturing. It buys up the entire industry's supply of denim and the copper rivets used on the pockets. Amazon acquires the largest cutters and sewers. Amazon will be the low cost provider with the best quality and deliver either the same day or the day after. Competitors will have no choice but to creep into the night, never to be heard from again.

For municipal bond investors the safest way to protect your portfolio from being Amazoned is to stay out of geographic areas where its decisions can adversely affect the issuer. These include:

- Over concentration of municipal revenue resulting directly or indirectly from Amazon
- Significant property taxes related to malls and other properties whose tenants compete against Amazon. Retail vacancies as of July 2018 are 10.2%—the highest since 2012

For corporate bond investors, avoid issuers competing head to head with Amazon. Examples **to stay away from** are Bed, Bath & Beyond; Macy's; Snap-on Tools; and Best Buy. All these bond issuers may potentially lose against Amazon and so will their bondholders.

* * *

Chapter 2: Unfunded Pensions

The American Legislative Exchange estimates US consolidated state and local unfunded pension liabilities at over $6 trillion—$50,000 for every American household. The problem, according to an analysis done by Illinois-based Wirepoint, is the growth of anticipated pension benefit payouts. These are rising far faster (about 200 percent faster, says Wirepoint) than the economies in 12 states. Naturally, New Jersey, Illinois, Connecticut, New Hampshire, and Kentucky lead this pack of financial misfits.

The answer is not to raise taxes. No state could possibly raise taxes enough to catch up with the growth of its pension benefits liabilities. The answer, says Wirepoint, is to rein in current worker benefits. That is something a few states, counties, and cities are now trying to do. We think it is too little, too late.

What's the danger to bonds?

Unfunded pensions are a liability to a municipality. They reduce the overall credit worthiness of the city, county, or state. New Jersey is a good example of a bad state. Their 2018 budget included a $3.2 billion pension contribution. A big number to be sure. But still only 60 percent of the actuary's computed minimum contribution. This shortfall triggered 11 credit ratings downgrades and tanked the bonds.

Four things cause pension underfunding:

1. Not making required pension fund payments
2. The fund's managers over estimate of returns they can achieve
3. Underestimating pension payouts
4. Cost of new benefits and the interest cost on the unfunded pension debt itself

No safe haven

It used to be that General Obligation bonds and some revenue bonds were immune from the risks of a severely unfunded pension municipality. Not any more.

In many cases, when faced with the dilemma of defaulting on liabilities and other obligations such as pension funds, the municipality simply raises more taxes, takes money out of the general fund, or invades the revenue stream from certain of its revenue bonds. This was once thought to be impossible. Now the impossible has become possible.

General Obligation bonds were once thought so safe. Now, taxpayers are already taxed to the max. Either they are protesting at the polls and voting the incompetents out of office or they're moving to less confiscatory states and taking their checkbooks with them.

The public demands a benefit from the taxes they pay. Using these tax increments to close the funding gap on retiree's pensions gives absolutely nothing to the current taxpayers. Another reason for them to pick up and leave. Why pay for someone else's mistakes?

Either way, the GOs from states, counties, and cities having severely unfunded pensions are at risk. At Envision Capital we know who the big offenders are and steer our clients clear of their GOs and most of their revenue bonds.

When the unthinkable happens

The unthinkable happens when a public pension plan declares itself insolvent. When (not if) this happens, there is no longer sufficient cash available to meet current obligations. The pensioners depending on that monthly check will soon be looking into an empty mailbox. Forever.

In our opinion, it is more likely that the entire municipality along with the pension fund both become insolvent at the same time. There would be no money anywhere to shore up the financial ship. Neither the municipality nor the pension fund could meet their obligations. But this is a very slow train wreck. Like the City of Detroit's insolvency. Observers saw this one coming for years. Astute bond investors had plenty of time to get out. The same is true of Puerto Rico.

What will cause this insolvency? Absurdly rich pension contracts negotiated by the public employees unions and agreed to by politicians more concerned with their own reelection than in doing the job they were hired to do in the first place. One example is Joe Robertson, the retired head of Oregon Health & Science University. Joe takes home a pension of $76,111 every month—over $900,000 annually. Then there's former University of Oregon head coach and athletic director Mike Bellotti. His generous pension gives off over a half million annually in benefits.

These contracts and thousands more like them will soon cause massive pension fund insolvencies.

How do investors protect themselves? Steer clear of the worst states. That's exactly what we at Envision Capital do for our clients. Today we have a list of states that are on the path to insolvency. Leading this list are Connecticut, Illinois, Kentucky, and New Jersey. We won't touch a General Obligation bond in any of these states and others.

Beware Pension Obligation Bonds

These are bonds issued by a state or municipality with unmanageable unfunded pension liabilities. Pension managers (who have already failed once to meet their investment target) are betting they can invest the bond proceeds at a higher rate than the bond coupon paid to the bondholders. If that were to happen they will pay the profit back into the pension fund to reduce the unfunded liability. Or so the theory behind POBs says.

This creates an enormous risk for the POB investor. What happens if the pension manager fails to make a profit investing the bond proceeds? Now the fund has dug an even deeper hole for itself.

We think equally likely, what happens if/when the municipality diverts the POB proceeds to pay for other operating expenses? Some may say that this won't happen…we know better. Detroit and Puerto Rico are the poster children for many of these bad deeds. We've seen some strange things in our 39 years in this business. Stay clear of pension obligation bonds.

* * *

Chapter 3: Confiscatory Taxation of Americans

Confiscatory. It's an odd word. One dictionary we consulted nailed its definition: *Being or imposing an excessive or unreasonable tax or cost.* Yep, that's it. Taxation comes in many forms. Here are some of the more offensive taxes and how they affect your bond portfolio.

State and local government's nasty habit

Taxing authorities allocate spending dollars to those who will reelect them. Likewise, they assess taxes to pay for this largess on those who are least likely to cause an interruption to their elected service.

The worst of state and local government's nasty habits is foregoing the actuarially mandated funding of employee's pension and healthcare plans in favor of spending the money elsewhere. Every year this goes on, the hole gets deeper. Soon there is no turning back.

California's communications tax

This is a new tax levied on cell phone lines, landlines, and other communications conveyances. The California state legislature is shooting for a $.34/line tax. It doesn't sound like much but estimates are this tax will generate $175 million in incremental revenue per year for this confiscatory state.

If passed, this tax will most likely expand in the coming years. Experts see it raising taxes on already overtaxed Californians by $500 million annually. Beware of creeping taxes that begin as minor but end up adding to an already overburdened electorate.

How you pay your estimated tax matters

Again, California leads the parade of greedy states. California requires all taxpayers making estimated or extension payments over $20,000 for a taxable year to use its electronic Web Pay system. This has a negative three-fold impact on California taxpayers:

1. It squeezes any float from the system. As soon as a taxpayer presses that button to complete the payment—BAM—the money leaves the account and flows directly to the State's coffers.
2. It is a perfect generator of fines and interest for the State. Exclusive use of Web Pay is a relatively new requirement. California taxpayers are now fined if they don't pay their tax estimates using Web Pay. The States waits a while before notifying them that their payment method was unacceptable. By that time, the unwitting taxpayer has already incurred a penalty for failing to pay the estimated tax due on time, *and* they have incurred interest charges as well. What a racket!
3. California no longer allows payment to the exact penny. Instead, they require taxpayers—through the Web Pay system—to round up their payments to the nearest dollar. Sounds minor, doesn't it? But beware that the State in its unquenchable thirst for tax dollars to squander, just may refuse payment in its entirety if rounded down, fine the taxpayer for untimely payment and start the interest clock running on the full amount. Lastly, the State gets a windfall in un-owed taxes by the amount of the rounding up of payments.

What SALT did

The State And Local Tax (SALT) component of President Trump's tax legislation eliminated states' ability to socialize their irresponsible excess costs to the taxpayers of other states. Here's how it works: There is now a cap on state tax deductions limited to $10,000. Suddenly states can no longer increase taxes knowing that however much they charge it's all deductible at the federal level and not completely payable by their constituency in hard dollars. With SALT, now those who actually have to pay the hard dollars are holding the state taxing authorities accountable for 100 percent of their tax increases.

Taxing devices

There are several methods taxing authorities employ to get around the laws limiting taxation of individual citizens. Here are a few.

Millionaire's tax

This tax ignores the fact that there actually have to be millionaires still living in the state to pay the millionaire's tax. The fact is millionaires are leaving the high-tax blue states in numbers significant enough to actually shift the balance.

An example is Illinois, infamous for its fiscal mismanagement and unfunded public employee pension plans. Over the last four years the state's GDP rose just 0.9% per year, half the national average. They attempted to make up for that with a series of tax increases. The result was that Illinois lost $18.35 billion in adjusted gross income to other states—the direct result of wealth out-migration.

Many of these so-called taxable millionaires file their taxes on the *individual side* of the tax forms, not on the corporate. So when they leave the high-tax blue states, they take with them their prosperous companies and their employees.

The delusional liberal interest groups don't know that at some point the wealthy and productive citizens will have enough and git while the gittin's good.

Head tax

These are based on the number of employees on the company's payroll. There have been a few cities that levied head taxes. Denver has a head tax. Chicago used to, but public outcry required them to repeal it. Pittsburgh taxes total employee compensation—a quasi head tax. Seattle, famous for its coffee, tried assessing a head tax twice but repealed it both times after strong opposition from Amazon and other large employers. As of this writing, two California cities—Mountain View and Cupertino—are considering a head tax.

Parcel tax

Cities that cannot live within their budget and refuse to reduce or cut non-essential services have adopted parcel taxes as a back door around the laws governing property tax limits. Parcel taxes are usually a flat fee levied on each property parcel within the taxing authority's boundaries.

Up to now, they're used to pick up the excess expenses (like unfunded teacher's pension and healthcare plans) from irresponsible school districts. However, more recently some more creative cities are using them to pay for many other things.

Here's an example of how we see the parcel taxed abused. The City of Palos Verdes Estates, California sits on the bluffs overlooking the Pacific. Its residents were threatened and browbeaten into voting for a parcel tax generating $45 million over nine years to fund the city's police department.

As with so many of these parcel taxes, we expect Palos Verdes Estates to fritter this money away—not on police services as promised, but on operating expenses and increased contributions to the unfunded police pension fund. Neither has anything to do with police services.

Indirect taxes

Tax authorities have learned that people seem to complain less about taxes they cannot see. Philadelphia understands this and uses it against its citizens. They are contemplating (at the time of this writing) to levy a new tax on real estate developers. These developers, of course, will pass the tax on to those who buy their buildings, homes, or rent from them. The poor citizens never see the tax, yet they're being assessed surely as if it were an income tax. It's the perfect crime—the victim doesn't know they've been hosed or who did it.

There are also the favorite discretionary taxes: Liquor taxes, cigarette taxes, marijuana taxes, and gambling taxes. The theory is that you don't have to do these things. You *want* to do them. So you should pay up.

Wealth is portable

According to the American Legislative Exchange Council in its 11th annual edition of *Rich States, Poor States,* about 3.5 million Americans have relocated from the highest-tax states to the lowest tax states over the past decade. This has produced an increase of $50 billion in income and purchasing power in Texas and Florida (no-tax states) and a loss of $23 billion in California and New York (the two highest taxing states). This is a fiscal bloodbath for the blue states.

If this confiscatory taxation doesn't stop, in the coming years millions of taxpayers, thousands of businesses, and tens of billions in net worth will flee high-tax blue states for the low-tax red states. President Trump's tax bill cap on the deductions for state and local taxes (SALT) has accelerated this pace. Those states losing their highest taxpayers are most of the Northeast and California. States getting the bounty of these wealthy citizens include Arizona, Nevada, Tennessee, Texas, and Utah.

Our recommendation: Do not invest in many of the General Obligation bonds from the confiscatory Blue States unless they are very short term. We expect the trend of wealth out-migration to increase.

* * *

Chapter 4: Concentration Comes in Many Forms

Bond investing requires a global view of not only the economy and interest rates but also much more. It requires appreciation of all things that could affect the issuer's ability to repay the bonds and to make timely interest payments to the bondholders. Here are the ones to which we pay the most attention.

Airport revenue bonds

At 93 of the top 100 US airports, just two airlines control a majority of the passenger traffic. What happens to that airport's revenue stream if one or both of these airlines either chooses to leave or encounters major headwinds and reduces operations?

This is the reason we don't recommend smaller airports as issuers of airport revenue bonds. The concept is good, but the over reliance on market share and just a few carriers ratchets up the risk. We are not in the risk business and neither are our clients.

An example is the City of Dayton, Ohio's $75 million airport revenue bonds. Dayton has lost enplanements each year to the Cincinnati and Columbus airports. Southwest Airlines recently closed its Dayton operations center. Neither is good for the airport's revenue prospects.

Dayton International's metrics show a steady decline in debt coverage ratios and airline subsidies paid to the airport. These resulted in a credit downgrade by Fitch. Such things combine to make any astute bond investor land at an alternate airport if they want exposure to airport revenue bonds.

Airport bonds we recommend include the majors: Los Angeles, San Francisco, Dallas/Fort Worth, and Hartsfield-Atlanta are just four on our list. Stick with the big boys that have significant and growing enplanements and stable financials.

Over reliance on one company or industry

Small municipal issuers too often find themselves at the fiscal mercy of a single industry or, worse, a single company. If that one industry or company falls on hard times, then the issuer's ability to service its bond debt becomes suspect. The bond prices fall, though rarely do the issuers actually default.

Take the case of Monroe, a city of just 20,000 people south of Detroit. The city's major revenue source comes from property taxes garnered from DTE Energy Company. Monroe will see 25 percent of its total revenue wiped out should DTE prevail in the appeal of its property tax bill for its coal-fired power plant. While the appeal is in process, the city must continue paying on its $45.4 million in outstanding General Obligation bonds. Monroe—and its bond investors—allowed an over concentration of just one company. Now they're paying the price.

Consider the bonds issued by the Central Greene, Pennsylvania School District (CUSIP: 153560QH3). These bonds are issued in a county whose 2016 assessed property value is hugely skewed toward the coal industry. In fact, 76 percent of the property in the area belongs to coal industry companies. Any blip down in the price of coal will send these companies scurrying to the tax appeals board.

They'll win favorable settlements because of the enormous clout they carry as a whole. Greene has no choice but to accept their terms. Most likely this will be detrimental to the bondholders.

The City of Detroit collapsed into bankruptcy after decades of seeing its population shrink as auto-industry jobs disappeared. Atlantic City, New Jersey found itself in the same pickle as a majority of its casinos either shuttered their doors and/or appealed their property tax assessments.

The petro chemical industry has the Houston coast in a worried state. Its fortunes are so closely linked to the price of oil and natural gas that any prolonged decline will affect the bonds issued in the area.

Exit King James

Do you remember back when Cleveland Cavaliers' star point forward was Lebron James? Then he left (again) this time for the sunny climes of Southern California and the Los Angeles Lakers. This was highly unfortunate for a variety of interests: Cavs owner, Dan Gilbert, was one. He extended the Cavaliers' lease on Quicken Loans Arena by seven more years in anticipation of another NBA championship like the one in 2016 led by James. The County of Cuyahoga and the City of Cleveland were left on the hook, guaranteeing the $140 million in bonds issued to upgrade and modernize Quicken Loans Arena where King James *used* to play.

Those owning the bonds discovered there was an over concentration and dependence on just one man—Lebron James. With the Cav's biggest draw fleeing to Los Angeles there is a risk that attendance may dwindle and that those guaranteeing the bonds may be required to step up and make them good. Or not, and leave the bondholders holding the bag. For this single player move, season ticket prices for the Los Angeles Lakers soared from $3500 to $6000. We assume they moved equally and in the opposite direction for the Cavaliers.

One huge cost

Once again, it seems the greatest cost to so many states, counties, and cities is unfunded pension liabilities. This certainly is the devil itself for Illinois. Pension costs account for 15 percent of the state's aggregate fixed costs. And this line item is growing every year as more people retire and their benefits increase according to their public employees union contract. In fact, pension costs are growing faster than Illinois' organic tax revenue growth.

Overcoming over concentration

Here's how we avoid bonds that rely too heavily on any single success factor:

1. Be skeptical. Identify what can go wrong with that bond's repayment revenue stream. Then determine the likelihood of that happening.
2. Identify the things the issuer is counting on to make its required revenue. It might be an airline continuing to use the airport. It could be the price of energy supporting the single industry in the area. It could be a

single person as in the case of the Cavaliers' franchise player who left for greener pastures.
3. Determine if there's any single huge cost that is rising out of control or at least faster than the area's organic growth. The first place to look is the pension costs. If the issuer is at the mercy of such a cost, pass on the bond.
4. Look at the Official Statement and the financials. The quickest way to remove a potential bond from your shopping list is seeing expenses outstrip income. For municipal bonds you can find this information on the eemma.msrb.org website.
5. What if the issuer hasn't published audited financial statements for a few years? Pass on the bond. Faith is something reserved for church, not our client's investments.

* * *

Chapter 5: Shots Fired in Treasury Market

What's the difference between the Federal Reserve and the US Treasury? Sometimes the relationship is blurred since the Fed and the Treasury work so closely together. Here's the difference:

The Department of the Treasury keeps America's checkbook. It collects taxes and manages US government revenues. The Treasury also prints currency and mints coins.

The Federal Reserve, on the other hand, is America's central bank. Its task is to, *"keep our money valuable and our financial system healthy."* It does this by influencing monetary policy. When the Fed acts responsibly and predictively, it ensures lenders and borrowers have access to money and credit. The Fed adjusts the discount rate and federal funds rate, keeping inflation at a desired level.

What about a possible credit crisis?

During the 2008 credit crisis many do-it-yourself investors saw their bond portfolios get nuked because of their over allocation in bank/financial bonds and auto bonds.

How and why did so many people make the same mistake? The simple answer is greed and inattention. At that time financial institution debt provided a higher yield than other debt sectors. Investors were greedy. They loaded up the boat with financials. Plus, the financial institutions were the largest issuers of bonds. Some we talked to insisted that their bond portfolio was safely diversified—they owned 5% in Citigroup bonds, 15% in Goldman Sachs, and 25% in Bank of America bonds.

This strategy may have insulated them from *issuer* risk but not from *sector* risk. It turned out that the credit crisis devastated the entire financial sector. Those with an over concentration in the financial institutions suffered pain, anguish, and losses.

Fast forward to the oil crisis in 2016. Oil related companies were [and still are] among the biggest bond issuers in the market place. Again, the need for yield won over common sense. For too many bond investors over concentration on a single sector proved a death knell for their bond portfolios. Oil prices hit the skids in 2016. Oil companies suffered greatly along with their bondholders.

What's the right allocation?

We advise our clients to keep allocations in any single company's bonds—no matter what the yield—to a maximum of 3-5%. For an industry group or sector, limit your exposure to a 10-15% allocation in your bond portfolio.

If you also own bond funds, you need to be extra careful. The bond fund probably also owns at least the same industry group or sector that you've limited your allocation to 10-15%. It may also own many of the single names you've limited your allocation to 3-5%.

Add the bond fund's allocation to your own allocation limits to be certain you haven't over allocated to a single name or industry group/sector. It may take some work on your part, but it is time well spent in case of an unforeseen crisis.

The Fed is reducing its balance sheet

This is no secret. The Fed is allowing outstanding Treasury bonds to roll off without replacing maturing bonds with newly issued bonds. The experts who track this forecast runoff expect it to grow to $50 billion per month by the end of 2018 and $600 billion during 2019. Some say this debt runoff, combined with the trillion-dollar annual deficits caused by tax cuts and increased spending could foreshadow elevated long-term interest rates.

This is important to bond investors who want to adjust their portfolios according to anticipated interest rate movements. Rising interest rates makes the already existing Treasury debt more onerous for America. The so-called trade war between the US, China, and Europe does not help the situation, and may foretell rising inflation. Both cause bond investors to worry about what might happen.

Since 2009 the Federal Reserve inflated and expanded its balance sheet. That inflated all assets—stocks, bonds, and real estate. Reducing its balance sheet will have the opposite effect—asset prices will drop. This seriously worries us.

Keeping our Asian creditors happy

China and Japan own the lion's share of America's Treasury debt—$1.2 trillion and $1.0 trillion respectively. America depends on both countries to fund its debt. What if one or both dump these massive holdings or if they suddenly refuse to attend the Treasury auctions? This would cause a rout in the bond market.

As of this writing, America and China are posturing around with trade tariffs. One side initiates a new tariff. The other side counters with one of their own. Neither side is happy. Chinese Ambassador to the US, Cui Tiankai has stated, "If the other side (that would be America) makes a wrong choice, we have no alternative but to fight back."

Fighting back by either side could be restricted to trade tariffs. Or it could escalate to economically weaponized Treasury debt. Our opinion is that we have a tough, experienced negotiator in President Trump. He understands negotiating leverage and [unlike past Administrations] is unafraid of using it. We say, go get 'em, Mr. President. If it comes down to winning or losing, America needs to win. It's about time America's leader showed some backbone.

Consequences of China reducing its US Treasury purchases

China has a lot of money it must deploy somewhere. Should China decide to reduce its US Treasury holdings, it would likely just replace them with other US assets. Our assets are the safest and most profitable investments out there. Net capital flow from China to the US would probably not change.

Interest rates in the US would not likely change much either. This trade-off of asset purchases would simply move China from less risky investments into those that are more risky.

China dumping US Treasurys or simply no longer buying them has significant consequences for China. They would be shooting themselves in the foot. We see China's implied threats against US Treasury bonds as the hollow musings of a paper tiger.

The bottom line with any shots fired in the Treasury market is this:

1. Pay attention to what actually happens and less to threats
2. Watch bond yields to get an indication of where the economy is going
3. Carefully adhere to your allocation discipline—3-5% to any single name and 10-15% to any sector or industry
4. Do not panic. The bond market rarely suffers from huge instant moves
5. Monitor the news on the flow of Treasury and agency securities in and out of the United States. This is found in the US Department of Treasury Resource Center at the www.treasury.gov website

* * *

Chapter 6: The negatives of corporate-issued debt

Companies have taken on huge debt burdens. The financial media calls these less-than-investment grade bond issuers, *the titans of junk*. Elon Musk at Tesla is one such titan. Michael Dell became another when he obtained huge risky loans to buy out the activists who threatened his control over Dell.

Those are just two borrowers constantly in the public's eye. Other huge private borrowers include Avantor, Inc., the specialty-chemicals maker, and the IT firm, BMC Software, Inc. The bulge in corporate issuance includes plenty of investment grade names too.

Over the last decade low interest rates and the corporate borrowing frenzy created a fervor. Mutual funds and ETFs grew fat and happy. Money kept rolling in. During the past five years corporate America issued approximately $9.2 trillion new bonds. According to the Dallas Fed, $3.5 trillion of that bond money went for share repurchases. Insurance companies bankrolled many of these leveraged buyouts.

Corporate benefit from the cash inflow of bond issues too often falls short of its cost. Financing mergers and acquisitions is one area that suffers greatly from over promising and under delivering. Often acquirers issue bonds to finance their acquisitions. Then they pay themselves fat dividends while letting the acquired company limp along, attempting to service the huge debt load without any benefit whatsoever from the money raised.

This massive amount of bonds was issued over the past several years to satisfy just one constituency—the shareholders. Issuing bonds for share repurchases (to reduce the amount of shares outstanding, thus increasing the earnings per share) or to increase dividends does nothing for the corporation's growth prospects or its profitability. Fast forward to sometime in the future when the economy slows down. That's when the trouble begins. Tons of corporate debt to pay interest in a declining or recessionary environment equals weaker debt service coverage, credit downgrades, and lower bond prices. Bottom line: Beware of bloated balance sheets.

Reading the fine print

There's a wrinkle that has made at least one type of bond offering seem like a slam-dunk for corporate investors. But not so much for individuals. It's called a *special mandatory redemption* (SMR). This feature was used to great effect by CVS in financing its acquisition of Aetna. The SMR details are important to understand. They required CVS to call back the bonds at 101 that were sold to finance the deal if it fell apart. CVS' bond deal was three times over subscribed due in large part to the attached SMR.

This was a good deal for the institutions that bought the original issue of these bonds. They would have made a small profit and had a ready buyer if the acquisition failed to occur.

Here's the problem for the individuals who may have bought these bonds on the secondary market. They had to buy them at a premium over the 101 buy back price. Had the deal cratered and the SMR kicked in, the individual investors would have suffered a capital loss—the difference between their premium purchase price and the 101 SMR buy back price. They would have no control over selling or not selling. Details like this can impact your bond portfolio when dealing with M&A.

The fallacy of add-backs

The leverage used in M&A deals climbed from 6.4 times EBITDA in the first quarter of 2015 to 7.7 times during the first quarter of 2018. Even these leverage increases may be suspect as accounting add-backs make the loans even more risky. Here's how it works.

The add-back adjustments increase earnings projections used to convince potential lenders that their loans are actually safer than they look. The add-backs occur when cost savings and/or revenue increases are figured into the financial projections as a result of the merger or acquisition. They haven't occurred yet. But they might. Or they might not. Lenders are more willing to take this possibility of such M&A success as a given that will keep their leverage ratios within the safety limits and allow them to make a loan that they otherwise would not have.

An example is the previously mentioned specialty-chemicals maker and supplier to the biotech and healthcare industries, Avantor, Inc. Backed by private equity firm, New Mountain Capital, LLC, they borrowed $7.5 billion to fund acquisition of VWR Corp. Avantor told its lenders that the combined company would generate $1 billion in EBITDA annually.

The problem was that half of this windfall came from *anticipated* cost savings and increased revenues. For example, a large part of the $1 billion EBITDA assumed the company could convince VWR customers to buy Avantor's products instead of competitors'. When this pie-in-the-sky add-back was removed, the leverage ratio soared to nine times EBTIDA (computed by Moody's). Such a risky loan does not belong in any individual's portfolio.

The practice of using add-backs allows lenders to green light loans that are actually outside the realm of reasonable safety limits. These loans are snapped up by funds and ETFs that individual investors buy into.

How to buy corporate bonds

First, evaluate the bond issuer's credit. Beware of over levered companies. Ask what could go wrong and how likely is that to occur? If you're considering a mutual fund or an ETF, study the credits in the portfolio. Determine the duration of the bond portfolio and figure out what happens to your holdings if interest rates rise or fall. You can also look at the issuer's credit rating by Moody's, S&P, and Fitch, though we don't usually put much credibility in those. Use the ratings only as a suggestion.

* * *

Chapter 7: Everybody into the Bond Indexing Pool
The indexing tsunami

A bond index fund or ETF is a portfolio of bonds that seeks to track the performance of a market index, such as the Bloomberg Barclays US Aggregate Bond Index. Bond index funds and ETFs give a portfolio control over geographic concentration, duration, and help manage sector exposure. Bond indexing is now sweeping through the bond market.

However, they also leave you completely exposed to the knee-jerk and hysterical reactions of other investors. When they panic, the bond index funds and ETFs will tank fast—often before most investors can get out. Picture a herd of panicked cattle storming the stockade's single, small gate. Only a few will get out unscathed. Those left behind will be trampled.

There's another negative associated with bond index funds. There is no final maturity for your investment. Those who own individual bond issues always know when the pain will end—that happens on the maturity date. They get their face value out and, if interest rates have increased, they can redeploy that capital into more profitable bond positions.

Not so for bond indexes, ETFs, and open-ended bond funds. Some investors either can't get out when they know they should, or insist that the fund will recoup its losses someday. That someday may be a long way off. Meanwhile, the fund value keeps falling.

Undue concentration

The difference between stock and bond funds lies in what each holds. Equity index funds own those stocks that track a specific index. They reward success. Fixed income indexes, on the other hand, favor those issuers with the most debt outstanding. This affinity for rapacious borrowing is no indicator of financial stability or future success.

All passive or quasi-active bond funds invest in companies that have the largest asset bases and the most substantial revenues to service that debt load. Nice words. However, by definition the bond funds usually buy a concentration in specific industries. When that industry hits the skids, the fund sinks into oblivion.

An example is BlackRock's iBoxx (HYG) bond fund. Here's the description they provide:

"The investment seeks to track the investment results of the Markit iBoxx® USD Liquid High Yield Index (the "underlying index"). The underlying index is a rules-based index consisting of liquid, U.S. dollar-denominated, high yield corporate bonds for sale in the United States."

During the financial crash of 2008 and 2009. It didn't matter how well diversified HYG was—or any bond fund, for that matter. Investors sold into the panic and lost their shirts. Had these same investors owned the individual bonds instead of the bond fund, they would have been able to exit whole when their bonds matured, assuming the issuers they held remained in business.

The point being, your portfolio of individual bonds may already have adequate coverage and exposure in the fund's concentration of the moment. Further, the fund almost certainly owns the biggest debt issuers in the chosen sectors. These may not necessarily be the issuers you wish to own. In this case, one size does not fit all. In our opinion, most fixed income investors are better off owning individual bond issues rather than bond funds and ETFs. Yes, it's more work. But individual bonds offer better predictability of an investor's income stream and we know exactly when any and all maturities will occur.

Indexing defenses

Not all bonds trade every day, as do stocks. This makes creating an index problematic. That's a nice word that means the bond fund portfolio managers are guessing as to which bonds to include in their index. They call this, *stratified sampling*. They make the assumption that bonds with similar characteristics will have similar risk attributes.

For example take a basket of BBB-rated telecom bonds with 7-10 years to maturity. Stratified sampling makes the assumption that all these bonds will perform similarly even as interest rates and spreads change. The portfolio manager assumes that selecting bonds from this grouping gets them the same risk factor as if they bought all the bonds in this index.

However, this strictly mathematical analysis for bond selection omits all the variables that happen every day in the real world. Things like management shake-ups, using bond proceeds for stock repurchases and dividend payouts, and outside business catastrophes.

How to defend yourself? We usually say to most investors who ask, stay away from the bond indexes. Instead just buy (or hire a money manager specializing in fixed income investments) individual bonds from issuers that one researched and monitored. This gives you the most precise control over geographic concentration, duration, and sector exposure.

However, there are those investors who really want to own bond indexes and ETFs. That's fine if you watch what the fund is doing. Here's how:

1. Research the fund's holdings to be sure that:
    a. These are issuers that you want to own
    b. The duration matches your overall objectives and interest rate risk tolerance
    c. The sectors owned by the fund are within your risk tolerance
2. If you buy a fixed income fund, be sure to constantly watch its value, its inflows, and outflows. If the value is dropping precipitously or there seems a large and sudden trend toward outflows, then get out. Don't wait. We do not want you to be the cow at the end (or even in the middle) of the stampede to get out. Be among the first to see the writing on the wall and leave.

* * *

Chapter 8: Technological Disruptors

Artificial intelligence as a disruptor

If the corporate bond issuers you own don't keep up with AI, then they will be overrun by competitors that do. Your bond values will fall. Both Western Union and Pitney Bowes are examples of companies succumbing to the competitive advantages of AI. Their stock is at an all time low in the longest bull market in history

AI is expanding over twice as fast as the other high-growth areas of technology—even faster than the cloud, big data, and security software. Among the fastest AI growth areas are personal digital assistants (Apple's Siri, Amazon's Alexa), analytics that drive operational efficiencies to new heights, natural language processing, and machine learning. The industries benefitting most are retail, healthcare, logistics, and financial services.

A recent study by PricewaterhouseCoopers estimated the potential economic contribution through AI by 2030 to be $15.7 trillion. They estimate that North America and China will receive 70 percent of this global GDP growth from AI.

Companies are using AI to increase sales, detect fraud, improve customer experience, automate work processes, and [accurately] do predictive analysis of customer behavior as well as that of financial instruments.

The retail sector is most susceptible to the dangers of ignoring AI and the enormous advantages of investing in its benefits. Customer recognition is a core competency that we believe will soon become the industry standard in retail. These are the chatbots, voice assistants, augmented-reality applications, and facial recognition technologies.

Such technologies have the ability to boost the sales of *existing customers*. Vendors such as Salesforce.com (Einstein), SAP (Leonardo), and Workday all use AI along with machine learning to recommend add-on sales to their existing customer base.

We see all of the above playing a pivotal role in next-gen retail sales and customer service. These capabilities are all data driven. It is like a fire hose streaming customer behavior data from outside third party gathering posts like Google, Facebook, Twitter, Snapchat, WhatsApp, and so many others. The retailers use AI to synthesize this stream of data, convert it to usable information, and then fire the results at customers in the form of tailored advertisements, recommendations, and suggestions. Already we hear cases of customers buying things suggested by Amazon's Alexa that they didn't even know they needed.

Four retailers investing in and partnering with AI technologies are:

- Best Buy has partnered with Amazon to offer products by the Alexa voice activation device.
- Microsoft has also partnered with Amazon to integrate both companies' virtual assistants—Cortana and Alexa.
- Google's Express partners with Wal-Mart for voice activated purchasing
- Target has partnered with Google Express, Home, and Android TV for voice activated purchasing.

'So what?' you ask. Your portfolio of corporate bonds should include companies whose management has already adopted to AI. Those refusing to recognize this tsunami of technology will ultimately be left in the dust.

Augmented reality as a disruptor

Amazon, IKEA, and Wayfair employ augmented reality in their home furnishings stores. This allows customers to actually *see* what furniture will look like in their own homes.

Another use of augmented reality is in the cosmetic space. Using the Sephora technology, customers can virtually apply make-up and see what they will look like.

New sales channels

Pop-up stores, micro-stores, and the instant access that social media provides are threatening established legacy retailers. This is just the latest assault on traditional brick and mortar stores already suffering at the hands of e-commerce giants like Amazon.

The Internet of things

This is coming fast. The Internet of things (IoT) is the network of physical devices, vehicles, home appliances, and other items embedded with electronics, software, sensors, actuators, and connectivity that integrates things from the physical world into computer-based virtual systems.

For example, your refrigerator may integrate into your Amazon Alexa device to automatically order more milk from Whole Foods (an Amazon company) and deliver it to your home. All before you realized your milk supply was low and without you even knowing that the purchase was done.

Another use of IoT is in the leisure industry. Disney Resorts, and many others (including some of the Las Vegas resorts) facilitate reservations, food orders, room access, entertainment, and payments using wearable devices. These come in the forms of wristbands, necklaces, and fobs carried in a pocket.

Embrace AI technology or die

Depending on the industry, there will be no choice but to invest in AI. The alternative is to die an uncontested death. When these slow-adapters or non-adapters die, the market won't even know they're gone.

Our take-away is this: Add debt-issuing companies to your bond portfolio that have demonstrated an aggressive investment and success with AI and with 5G technologies. These will be the future disruptors and market leaders. Their credit worthiness will continue to grow.

Avoid those companies that refuse to acknowledge the benefits of AI and 5G. These companies cannot compete against those that do. Their profits, cash flow, and credit ratings will decline.

The opportunity of 5G

As of this writing the latest technology wrinkle, 5G, is just being rolled out. The 5G communications technology reduces latency—the lag between when data is requested from the network and when it arrives at the use point, be it your phone, computer, or television. This technology shrinks latency from 50 milliseconds to just 1 millisecond. The difference may seem meaningless. Afterall, 50 milliseconds is just 50/1,000 of a second. Think again. With virtually no latency, people and machines can now communicate and transfer data simultaneously in real time.

Pay attention here. Some companies will benefit hugely from 5G technology. The cellular telephone manufacturers will sell new 5G phones, of course. The FCC Chairman estimates the need for 800,000 5G cell sites. So the cell tower companies and antenna manufacturing companies will be among the beneficiaries of this technology. Chipmakers, network gear suppliers, and software companies will see enormous upside from 5G.

Healthcare will also benefit. Suddenly, patients who once needed an extended hospital stay for monitoring can now go home. With 5G communications, their monitoring is instantaneous. The hospitals won't benefit since their revenue depends on occupied beds. But the insurance companies who pay the bills will absolutely benefit through cost reductions.

This will also benefit the robotics industry. By cutting latency to basically nothing (real time), applications that require perfect precision and instant feedback (such as surgery) can be done remotely using specialized robots.

Cable companies will see a majority of their customers cutting the cord. 5G wireless connections will provide reliable and instantaneous connections between TVs and other devices. All that's needed is a wireless router to get the services once only provided by cable at real time speeds.

The defense industry will see the benefits of 5G technology. Immediate feedback means that military operations can be controlled remotely, using drones with facial recognition capability. The enemy is identified and engaged all without any risk to our soldiers.

The gaming industry is another beneficiary. Casinos will become unnecessary. People can gamble on a wide variety of devices in real time anywhere.

The bond industry has been slow to react to 5G. As of this writing, the yields and spreads of some companies likely to suffer from the 5G rollout as well as those that will benefit have not moved—yet.

The best investors are those who observe the future and then act before it arrives.

* * *

Chapter 9: The bond binge is over—now what?

Interest rates worldwide have been limbo-low for a long time. That is the main reason for the massive debt issuance over the last decade. According to the Bank of International Settlements (BIS) debt worldwide has increased by over $60 trillion to its current level of $170 trillion. BIS says this debt level is 40 percent higher than just before the 2008 Lehman Brothers bankruptcy that caused the credit house of cards to topple.

For us, the final nail in the coffin of rising credit risk came from a McKinsey & Co. study that concluded two-thirds of corporate debt was issued by companies having a *significantly high risk of default*. No doubt this combination of soaring debt levels combined with compressed interest rate spreads, and declining credit quality is causing the world's central bankers to lose sleep at night.

The financial media calls this situation a *mispricing of credit risk*. In other words, the credit market has lost its discipline for correctly applying a rate for every risk. Instead, they are granting low interest rates for higher and higher credit risk and hoping everything works out. Fingers crossed, in other words. This is a bad idea.

Already we see advertisements for residential and auto loans offering no money down, a 100 percent loan to value ratio, and no proof of income required. Such subprime lending is exactly what caused the credit crisis of 2008-2009.

We now see the same toxic combination of high debt issuance, low interest rates, and mismatched credit risk. This is creating a credit bubble. All such bubbles eventually burst. Over the next four years $2 trillion *per year* of corporate debt is scheduled to mature. Can these companies either repay their debt in full or roll it over with new, more costly debt? For some, it's questionable.

These voracious borrowers contend that burgeoning corporate profits are more than enough to service the higher debt load. They also cite windfall proceeds from the tax overhaul and repatriated foreign cash as sources for use in debt repayment.

We don't believe it. Use of such proceeds for debt repayment requires an intestinal fortitude (balls, cojones, whatever you want to call 'em) that few corporate chieftains possess.

Some will say, 'but this time it's different.' We imagine these are the same people who issue large amounts of debt, then use the proceeds for stock buy-backs or to increase shareholder dividends. Neither provides the capital needed to improve the company that must service its debt.

This time is no different. Those insisting it is seem to forget a number of things. One is that the new tax rules limit the deduction of interest expenses on companies barely making any money. In itself, this is a tornado-like headwind for serial corporate borrowers. The bankruptcy courts will be busier than ever over the coming years.

Corporate bond risk

Investment grade corporate bonds (rated BBB- or better) typically have a longer time to maturity. Duration is a bond portfolio's sensitivity to interest rate changes. As interest rates rise, bond prices fall, and yield rises. A duration of 3 tells you if rates increase 1% immediately, your portfolio will decline about 3%. The longer the duration, the more sensitive bonds will be to interest rate gyrations.

Whether you are an open end, closed end, ETF, or a raw bond investor, knowing your bond duration mentally prepares you for the portfolio swings we are sure to experience. Remember too the rating agencies have one mandate: Make money for their company. It's not: Do an honest, honorable, accurate job of rating corporate and municipal bonds. Use their ratings only as a suggestion—nothing more.

Deteriorating credit quality

It's no secret that investment grade corporates are deteriorating in their credit quality. Here's the trend in numbers:

- During 2007 just 27 percent of the total value of bonds issued by companies in S&P's 500-stock index carried BBB ratings

- By 2018 this soared to 50 percent of the market value of S&P 500 bonds that are rated BBB. That's an 85 percent increase

Here's the bottom line regarding the bond binge: The quality trend is certainly downward. Know that credit quality of your present bond portfolio will deteriorate over the next cycle. What can you do to sustain your portfolio value?

1. **Invest in issuers that will not sacrifice their own business to improve short term EPS, through engineered stock price increases**
2. **Buy issuers that invest bond proceeds to improve their bottom line**
3. **Invest in funds or raw municipal bonds the majority of which are revenue bonds. This will help insulate you when the pension problems finally hit**

Follow these guidelines and you will only have paper cuts, not portfolio bleed-outs at the end of this raucous bond issuance spree. Be smart so that when the adjustment hits, your bond portfolio will barely feel it.

* * *

Chapter 10: Actionable Intel

Remember the convoluted description of unknowns attributed to former Defense Secretary, Donald Rumsfeld:

"There are known knowns. These are things we know that we know. There are known unknowns. That is to say, there are things that we know we don't know. But there are also unknown unknowns. There are things we don't know we don't know."

These same words are relevant in today's bond market. Perhaps when you began reading this your known knowns were many. Maybe we've clarified your known unknowns about bonds. Still it is the unknown, unknowns that can take down the bond market. It makes better sense if we break it down like this:

Known knowns

We all know a lot about the bond market. There are many cause and effect relationships between the economy, international relations, energy supply, and pricing, the list goes on. Here are just a few of our known knowns:

1. *Rate hikes:* All bonds except municipals have reacted to Federal Reserve interest rate hikes. That's because demand is far greater than the supply of munis offered for sale.
2. *Pension Obligation Bonds:* There's no more road down which politicians can kick unfunded pension liabilities. The day of reckoning is here. Stay away from Pension Obligation Bonds. Limit your exposure to General Obligation bonds issued by state, city, county, and school districts having massively underfunded pensions. Instead, stick with good quality municipal revenue bonds where the issuer provides essential services.
3. *Your place on the yield curve:* Stay at the front end of the yield curve (buy short maturities) if it's flat and go longer when it becomes positively sloped
4. *Iffy bond ratings:* Don't count on bond ratings to be accurate. If revenues exceed expenditures annually

35

with municipals, then take a chance. The same goes for corporates. Ratings are a moving target.
5. *Watch your brokers:* Be vigilant about the price you pay. Look at the mark-ups and markdowns on your bond buy/sell transactions. If they are too high, then change brokers.

Known unknowns

There are things that we know we don't know. In many cases they are unknowable. Yet, these same things will affect the bond market. We don't know when that inflection point will occur or by how much. Many would fluff off these known unknowns, saying so what? However, the bond market often moves slow enough to take action if you watch a surprise event unfold and know what action to take.

Bond investors know they need to watch for signs that an issuer is on the downswing. But they don't know which issuer that will be—a known unknown. The collapse of Puerto Rico is a good example. Puerto Rico is the poster child for fiscal mismanagement. Most certainly there were a myriad of warning signs years in advance of its collapse. Smart holders of Puerto Rico's bonds focused on this known unknown as soon as the signposts showed up. Suddenly Puerto Rico moved into the category of a known, known. Investors knew Puerto Rico was going down. Some sold their bonds without getting hurt. Others held on. Some will recoup only pennies on the dollar. Puerto Rico's collapse was like watching a train wreck in slow motion. Yet so many investors inexcusably lost their shirts.

Here are a few other things we know that we don't know about the bond market:

1. *Collateral damage:* A wobbly financial institution can cause collateral bond damage even if you don't own the particular wobbly name
2. *Contractual promises mean little:* Just because a state cannot declare bankruptcy under the law, it can still default on payments owed. Ring fenced, perfected liens, and pledged security can all be

breached when a municipality is in desperate financial trouble.
3. *Fortunes change:* Corporations have their ups and downs. In 2011 GE was rated AA+. It's now rated A- by S&P. We think it should be rated junk.
4. *Understand what you own:* Never think we managers have all the answers. All those municipal bond fund managers who rode Puerto Rico bonds all the way down were both arrogant and wrong to the extreme financial detriment of their clients.
5. *Trust your own judgment:* Don't believe the financial media's talking heads know any more about interest rate moves than you do. It is a quantitative guessing game the Fed often confuses, and the public usually mangles.

Unknown unknowns

These are the things we have no idea of and worse, that we don't know their affect on the bond market. But we know they're out there. Some call them black swan events—things so rare that they are off the radar screen—until they occur. At one time a terrorist attack on American soil was one of these. Not any more.

Here are a few examples of events that affected the bond market once categorized as unknown unknowns:

1. *Earnings restatements:* If a corporate executive announces an earnings restatement, sell the bonds. There is no way to know what is actually going on.
2. *Beware of M&A:* When mergers and acquisitions are announced it's unknown if the promises of synergies and cost reductions will ever come to fruition. Take your best shot at accessing the situation. If your bonds do not have a change of control covenant you may have to sell.
3. *Trust your common sense:* When something is happening below the radar—like the toxic mortgage bonds being rated and sold as AAA paper in 2008

that caused a financial crisis—take action on what you know. Don't just sit there. None of our clients lost their shirts.

4. *Make bonds your safety net:* The greatest unknown for Baby Boomers is how much time we have left. Don't squander it chasing Bitcoin-type dreams. Keep your bond portfolio simple and safe. There is no time left to make up for big blunders.

Specific actions for investors

Here's our list of the specific actions we take on behalf of our clients as the bond market changes:

1. *Don't let your portfolio be Amazoned*: Do not buy bonds issued by municipalities whose revenue comes either directly or indirectly from Amazon. Don't buy corporate bonds from issuers attempting to compete against Amazon…they will lose.
2. *Avoid unfunded pensions*: Know which states, counties, and cities have severely under funded pension plans and do not buy their bonds—not even the GOs or the revenue bonds. Four of the biggest problem states are Connecticut, Illinois, Kentucky, and New Jersey. There are others. And remember: The power to raise taxes is the same power to change the rules when times are tough.
3. *POBs*: Do not buy pension obligation bonds.
4. *Airport revenue bonds*: Do not buy bonds issued by smaller airports dependent on just a few airlines for their subsistence. Los Angeles, San Francisco, and Hartsfield-Atlanta airports are just three of the airport revenue bonds we like.
5. *Over dependence*: Do not buy municipal issuers that are too dependent on any one company or industry for their revenues.
6. *Maintain the proper allocation*: Limit allocation to any single company's bonds to a maximum of 3-5%.

Limit allocation to any single industry group or sector to 10-15% of your bond portfolio.
7. *Corporate bond issuance*: Beware of bloated corporate balance sheets when analyzing the suitability of their debt.
8. *Bond index funds*: Not our favorite.
9. *Buy into technology*: Buy bonds from companies with a demonstrated success and aggressive investment in artificial intelligence.
10. *The credit quality trend*: There's a downward trend in credit quality. Know that credit quality of your present bond portfolio will deteriorate over the next cycle. This will depress your portfolio's value.

* * *

About the authors

Marilyn Cohen

Marilyn Cohen is one of the country's top Bond managers. She began her 39-year financial career as a securities analyst at William O'Neil & Co. She moved into bond brokerage at Cantor Fitzgerald, Inc. then founded Envision Capital Management 23 years ago. As Envision's CEO, Marilyn and her company specializes in managing bond portfolios for individuals.

During this same 23 years Marilyn has written the bond column appearing in **Forbes** magazine, and has written five books about investing in bonds.

Marilyn is a popular guest on CNBC, Fox Business News, PBS and each of the major broadcast networks. Contact Marilyn at 800.400.0989 or by email at envision@envisioncap.com.

Chris Malburg

Chris Malburg is a widely published author. With over 5 million words in print scattered among 28 books and over 100 magazine articles, his work is consumed in most western countries. He writes on the subjects of management, business strategies, and financial terrorism (*God's Banker* and *Man of Honor*). He lives in Southern California with his wife where they are volunteer puppy raisers for Canine Companions for Independence (www.cci.org) and Guide Dogs for the Blind (http://www.guidedogs.com).

The authors with therapy dog, Dove, who volunteer at the VA Hospital and USO weekly

Connect with us online

Marilyn Cohen:
Website: www.Envision@EnvisionCap.com

Chris Malburg:
Website: www.WritersResourceGroup.com
Twitter: http://twitter.com/#!/ChrisMalburg
Facebook: http://facebook.com/chris.malburg
Linkedin: http://www.linkedin.com/in/chrismalburg

A final word from the authors

We hope you have learned from and enjoyed *Top 10 Bond Market Worries* and will profit from its lessons. We invite you to enter a review on whatever platform you purchased it. Just log in and give as many stars as you think our effort deserves. Finally, our readers are generous with their emails and tweets. We always make time to answer. If you wish to send us a note, you are welcome to send it to envision@envisioncap.com.

Best wishes,

Marilyn Cohen and Chris Malburg

Other books by Marilyn Cohen and Chris Malburg

The Great Unravel
The Little Bond eBook
Surviving the Bond Bear Market
Bonds Now!
Bond Bible

About Envision Capital

Minimum account size:	$500,000
Annual fees:	
Municipal bonds:	.43%
Investment Grade Corporates:	.60%
Split rated:	.75%
High yield:	1.00%

There are break points in fees depending on account size. Contact us for further details:
  Telephone: 800.400.0989
  Email: envision@envisioncap.com
  Address: 2301 Rosecrans Ave. Suite 4180
  El Segundo CA 90245